# Book 1
# Malware
**By Solis Tech**

&

# Book 2
# Quality Assurance
**By Solis Tech**

# Book 1
# Malware
By Solis Tech

***Malware Detection & Threats Made Easy!***

**Malware:** Malware Detection & Threats Made Easy!

# Table of Contents

**Introduction......5**

**Chapter 1 - Malware......6**

**Chapter 2 - Virus......10**

**Chapter 3 - Worm......12**

**Chapter 4 - Trojan Horse......15**

**Chapter 5 - Threats on Mobile Devices......20**

**Conclusion......22**

## Introduction

I want to thank you and congratulate you for purchasing the book, *"Malware: Malware Detection & Threats Made Easy!"*.

This book contains proven steps and strategies on how to avoid, detect and remove malware.

Malware creators are very creative, employing both technical and social means to spread malware. Simply installing antivirus software is no longer enough. This book explains how malware spreads in order to arm the reader with information on how to manage its threat.

Thanks again for purchasing this book, I hope you enjoy it!

# Chapter 1 – Malware

Computers are inherently dumb. They can accept and input data, can process it at high-speed, and can return the results almost instantly. However, users need to tell the computer what to do in the form of codes. We call these codes programs, applications, scripts or software, but they are essentially the same. They give instructions to the computer. What the computer does will depend on the instructions given to it. Tell it to do something useful and it will. Give it instructions to perform a malicious task and it will do it without question. Even computers with artificial intelligence are simply following instructions that simulate human's way of thinking.

Computers do not care who gives the instructions. As long as the instructions are loaded into memory, the computer will process it accordingly. Upon startup, a short set of instructions will tell the computer to load and launch the operating system or OS. The OS in turn executes startup instructions that it finds. These include preparing the input and output drivers, as well as launching other background tasks. Having done that, the OS awaits command from its user to execute other applications.

Malware developers take advantage of these key concepts. They find vulnerabilities in the operating and network system that will allow them to install malware and have it running in the background. Vulnerabilities are bugs in the program that can let malware writers load additional code and execute it. These bugs or programming errors do not always appear during the testing stage.

Some malware writers use social engineering to trick victims into installing malware into their computers. They use the computer's connection to internal and external networks to propagate the malware. They infect shared storage to spread malware among colleagues. They hack into servers to install malicious code that will infect site visitors. They can do this because computers will run any executable code that is loaded into its memory.

## What is Malware?

Malware is short for malicious software. It is a general term for a code that compromises a computer and instructs it to do malicious tasks, often without the knowledge or permission from the computer's owner. Early malware refers to programming challenges and pranks like programs that delete user files, but recent malware refers to targeting servers to make them inaccessible or for financial gains.

Home computers are not safe, either. Cybercriminals are using home computers to launch attacks on servers in addition to stealing personal information to access online bank accounts. Some advertisers adopt malware, too. They no longer wait for users to visit their sites, but install malware into a victim's computer so they can modify browser settings and change the default home page, eventually advertising their products every time a user opens the browser. They sometimes change the default search engine, replacing it with engines that track user habits to benefit advertisers.

Mobile devices are not safe, either. Today's mobile devices are computers with features and capabilities that are comparable to older computers. Mobile devices, like smartphones and tablets, are vulnerable because they require applications to work. If users inadvertently download a compromised application, then there is a possibility that malware can compromise their mobile devices, too.

A future malware playground is Internet of Things. It is a term for consumer devices like smart home appliances and vehicles loaded with small computers to provide intelligent functionality. These intelligent appliances connect to the Internet for remote control and administration. Having computers on these things, it may not be long until we can see malware on these devices too.

Remember that appliance manufacturers are not IT companies; hence, they may not have the capability to implement data security in their products. A hacker compromising a manufacturer's server could trigger a firmware update on connected appliances and make it perform additional functions, including attacking other servers on the Internet. It may sound like an event from a science-fiction movie, but this reality is possible.

## What is the Difference Between a Malware and a Virus?

Many people confuse malware with viruses. A virus is a type of malware, while malware include viruses and other malicious software.

The first malware were viruses, and developers wrote antivirus software to eliminate these malicious programs. Even when viruses evolved to other forms, people still call them viruses and antivirus companies are using the same term even if they are targeting other malware variants.

Viruses are no longer common on their original form. With antivirus vendors constantly updating their algorithms, malware developers have to come up with new variants to avoid detection, often employing social engineering to propagate malware faster by tricking victims to install it along with legitimate software.

If we look at how malware developers remain active over the years, we can surmise that it is a financially rewarding business; therefore, we can expect cybercriminals to continue developing better malware while antivirus companies play catch-up. The only way to combat malware is to understand the threat it presents, how it spreads and propagates, how to detect it, and how to remove.

## What are Potentially Unwanted Programs (PUPs)?

People love free software; however, developers need to earn money too. Malware developers see this as an opportunity to spread malware while providing revenue to free-software developers. What they come up with are installers for legitimate software that also install malware during installation. Antivirus companies call these Potentially Unwanted Programs instead of malware since victims give explicit permission to install them. They have no way of knowing if users allow the installation on purpose or unknowingly installs them.

### Why would Users Give Permission to Install PUPs?

Most users do not bother reading user agreements that installers display during installation. Instead, they simply click on the default buttons or press enter. Even if users will read the agreements and prompts, some may not understand the message and assume that they are installing software that is necessary for the main program to work. Unfortunately, PUPs are easy to install, but are often frustrating to remove from the system. Most have more than one instance running such that removing a copy will trigger the second copy to re-install it. Many recent PUPs affect users' browsers, which can be very annoying.

### How to Detect the Presence of Malware?

Users familiar with their computer will sometimes notice unusual behavior. Some are obvious, like the browser's looks suddenly changing. Other users may lose their files or the file types are changed. Users may even see system errors that were not present before.

Some changes are not visual, like a program accessing the hard disk and making noise even when the computer is idle. Malware accessing an external server can slow down Internet connection. Infected computers can also be unresponsive when hidden processes are running and using up the computer's memory.

Before assuming that malware may be causing the problem, try restarting the computer and leave it for a few minutes without running any program. If the computer is still slow, then there may be an unwanted background program running, but it still needs confirmation.

On Windows, check the hard disk space by opening any folder and clicking Computer on the left. A hard disk with very little space can slow down the computer and malware may not be the cause.

If there is plenty of hard disk space available, run the Task Manager by holding Ctrl+Alt+Del and selecting it from the menu. Click on the Performance tab and observe the real-time graph. Both the CPU and memory usage should be relatively flat if the computer is idle. An active graph could mean that a hidden program is busy. Click the Applications tab to confirm. There should be no application listed if the user did not execute a program. If there is no program listed and the CPU or memory graph is active then there could be a malware running in the background.

To see the process that is using up the memory, click on the Process tab, then click Memory to display the list in descending order. Check its Image name and description. Right-click on a name, then select Properties to get more details. Use a search engine to validate suspicious names.

The Networking tab can also give clues on the presence of malware. There should be no network activity if the computer is idle. If the network is slow and this graph is active, then a hidden program is accessing an external server or computer.

These are just some ways of detecting the possible presence of malware. Without knowing what the malware exactly is; however, it could be difficult to remove it manually.

Most leading antivirus software can detect and remove malware. For home users, there are free versions available that offer basic protection with the option to purchase upgrades for additional features.

## A Note on USB flash drives

With the popularity of USB flash drives, spreading malware via USB is easier. Malware can automatically execute when the user opens a USB flash drive. Once in computer memory, inserting another USB drive will infect it. To prevent this, do not view the contents of a USB flash drive after it mounts. Instead, right-click on the drive's name or icon, then select the scan option from the antivirus. This will remove malware in the flash drive before using it.

If there are signs that a USB drive is infected, but the antivirus does not detect it, install another antivirus program. Some antivirus solutions are not good at detecting USB-based malware.

Antivirus solutions can prevent the installation of malware to some extent. However, there are malware that can still get through if the user is not aware of how they propagate. The best way to prevent malware from infecting computers is to understand how each type works.

The succeeding chapters give an insight into the various forms of malware. It also provides information on how they spread so that users can avoid infecting their computers. Prevention is still the best cure against malware. However, avoiding malware is not easy.

# Chapter 2 – Virus

Viruses are the earliest forms of malware and they date back to the time before personal computers became popular. A virus is simply a program that can replicate itself on the same computer. Even without malicious intent, creating many copies of a virus code can quickly fill up the memory and slow the computer down. However, an unmodified virus cannot spread to other computers by itself even if the computers are on a network. Getting the virus inside a computer is the challenge for virus creators.

To avoid detection, virus creators modify legitimate programs by inserting malicious codes. When these programs launch, the virus loads into memory and scans the computer for other executable codes to infect. The virus code stays active in memory until the computer shuts down and the cycle starts again if the user runs the infected program.

### Boot Sector Virus

Some viruses attack the boot sector of the computer's bootable disks. The boot sector is an area of a disk that a disk drive initially reads and loads into memory. It contains the startup code that will load other components of the operating system. When the boot sector is infected, the virus loads into memory every time the computer starts, ensuring that it is active without waiting for the user to run an infected program. Since the disk operating system can fit in diskettes in the early days of personal computers, starting a clean computer with an infected bootable diskette can also spread the virus to that computer.

### Be Careful when Using Shared Resources

Viruses can spread through sharing. When a user mounts a removable storage media on an infected computer while a virus is active, the virus attempts to infect programs that it finds on the mounted media as well. In the early days, this applies to floppy diskettes and external hard drives, but infections are more common today on flash USB drives.

Once the user connects an infected storage to another computer and runs an infected program, the virus activates and infects the other programs in the new computer as well. This makes users who mount USB drives on shared computers at risk if the computer has no sufficient antivirus protection installed. For this reason, avoid connecting USB drives at Internet cafes and on other public computers.

Even shared documents can carry viruses. Some productivity software allows scripts or macros to automate common tasks. Scripts and macros are small, but powerful programs; hence, they can spread viruses, too. Executing an infected macro will also compromise other documents on the same computer. Worse, sending a copy of an infected document can also infect the receiver's computer.

### Are Early Viruses Malicious?

Some early viruses started as programming challenges. There was a game that was named Core Wars where the objective is to create a program that loads in memory, then replicate and terminate other programs running on the same memory space. The competing programs create copies of the code while overwriting enemy codes to terminate them. The program that remains in control is the winner.

Other early versions are simply annoying. Two programmers wrote the Brain virus because users were illegally copying their diskettes. The Brain virus simply displays information about the programmers. The Brain virus spread to computers in other countries.

Computers were not widely connected before and the worst thing that a virus can do is to delete files or make them inaccessible. This is exactly what early destructive viruses did. Some programmers wrote viruses that display something interesting while deleting computer files.

### Birth of Antivirus Companies

It was not long before other programmers started writing codes to remove viruses, turning the process into a never-ending game of cat and mouse. Virus creators are continually discovering new computer vulnerabilities that they can take advantage of, while antivirus developers update their codes to combat new virus strains. It has become a never ending battle between malware developers and antivirus companies.

Antivirus programs initially identify specific viruses using their signatures. Signatures are like patterns or fingerprints that identify specific viruses. Virus creators responded by continually creating virus variants that require new methods of detection to keep up. This is why antivirus programs update their databases almost daily.

Antivirus can only play catch up if they rely solely on signatures. Modern antivirus programs detect possible viruses by their behavior in addition to signatures.

Most free antivirus software in the market can eliminate common virus threats so not having one installed is not an excuse. While they retain the name, current antivirus software can detect and remove other forms of malware. To enable additional protection, users can purchase additional features.

However, those who do not have a budget for paid features can still protect themselves from malware. The key is to understand how other forms of malware spread. The next chapters will explain these.

# Chapter 3 - Worms

While viruses were a threat due to their ability to replicate, it is not a tool for mass infection because it cannot spread to other computers. The capability to spread over the network by itself is a feature of worms. Networks include local area networks (LAN) that are commonly found in offices, Wide Area Network (WAN) for remote offices, as well as worldwide networks like the Internet.

Early worm research had good intentions and started as helpful ideas. One worm crawls networked computers at night to run processor-intensive tasks, but saves the work and stays idle during the day so people can use the computers normally. It is a good idea that maximizes computer resources, similar to how modern cloud computing works. However, a programming error caused the computers to crash and they had to write another program to remove it.

Another programmer wrote a seemingly harmless worm to check the size of the Internet. The worm creates copies on target computers as it moved from one computer to the next. Due to a programming decision, it can install a copy even if it already exists on the same computer. Multiple running copies of the same worm can slow down the computer until it eventually crashes. A single worm was able to crash a big part the Internet.

Worms spread across the network by exploiting operating system and application vulnerabilities and taking advantage of insufficient data security practices. Nowadays, worms can also spread through social engineering. Social engineering is a technique used by hackers to trick users into unknowingly breaking standard data security precautions. Hackers can bypass a highly secure environment using social engineering.

Operating systems, or OS, are programs that manage computers and network equipment. Just like any program, it can have unintentional bugs and updating usually fixes the problem. Worms take advantage of these vulnerabilities to compromise the system.

If the OS or application developer releases an update before someone announces the vulnerability, then users have time to update the operating system before a malware exploits the vulnerability. This is why users should install updates especially if the patch is to address data security issues. Allowing automatic updates usually takes care of this, although there is a risk of automatically installing buggy updates.

On the other hand, if a malware creator releases a worm before the developer discovers the bug and releases an update, what we have is zero-day vulnerability. Modern antivirus companies address this by developing algorithms that detect malicious behavior. However, very aggressive antivirus solutions may lead to false positives.

False positives result when a scan reports the presence of malicious code when there is none. A good antivirus has few false positives. Third party evaluations can determine effective antivirus solutions with fewer false positives.

## Mass-mailer worms

Worms can access email clients on user computers and use it to email copies of the worm to contacts in the address book. Some of these emails can trick recipients into downloading and installing the attachment, compromising the receiver's computer in the process. When this happens, that computer also becomes a mass-mailing tool. Unfortunately, these worms can also get a name from the address book and change the From field with this name. This means that the sender in the email may not be the email source, making the source difficult to track.

Aside from possibly compromising recipients' computers, mass mailers can also slow down network performance. If a worm infects several computers on the same network, then it could eat up all the allocated bandwidth. Worse, data security companies may include the computer's IP address in the blacklist for spamming. This can affect all computers in the network that shares the same public IP.

This is because most offices and home networks use a single public IP address for their router while individual computers get private IP addresses. Worse, some DSL subscribers may get a banned public IP address when their router restarts.

Always be wary of unsolicited emails with attachment even if it comes from a trusted source. A possible indicator of spam mail is when the receiver's name is not mentioned in the salutation. Bad grammar is also a sign of possible spam email.

Do not assume that the antivirus can catch all worm variants. Some worms change the file extension of the attached file. Users may think that they are opening an image file when in reality they are executing a worm. Worms do this by adding a .jpg to the filename, like picture.jpg.exe. Since many users configure their computers to hide the file extension, they do not see that the real extension is .exe because the filename they see is picture.jpg.

Some mass-mailer worms simply send spam advertisements. While they may not do damage to a user's computer, they can still trick victims into purchasing illegitimate products. These emails often have a web beacon, a small image that is loaded from an external server. Displaying this image will send the user's email address to the server, thereby validating that it is an active email account. It will then be a target for future spam emails.

Note that spammers do not use their own computers to send mass emails. They use email worms to prevent authorities from easily tracking them.

## Worms for Phishing

Mass-mailer worms provide a great platform for quickly distributing malware. Malware creators use these worms to transport different payloads depending on their intention. One application of mass-mailers is for phishing.

Phishing is a form of identity fraud and is usually for stealing personal information for financial gains. It works this way.

Malware creators will copy a legitimate website's looks, specifically the login and profile pages. Websites of financial institutions like banks and payment platforms are examples of these. Next, they will create an email that looks like an official document coming from the target institutions. These emails often have a sense of urgency, requiring the user to log in to the website immediately to validate or change the password for security purposes. It will also include a link to the appropriate page for the user's convenience.

There lies the trick. Instead of linking to the legitimate page, it will redirect the user to the fake login page after clicking the email link. The URL will have the legitimate website's domain name, but with added characters. Some users may mistakenly believe that they are in the genuine site and proceed to log in. After entering the login detail, the next page may even require them to enter their credit card details for validation.

In reality, users can enter anything in the login page and it will be successful. The login page will simply save the credentials entered by the user, then display a page to get other credentials. When in doubt, users can initially enter incorrect login credentials to check if the site can really validate their account. If it accepts a wrong username or password, then there is no validation and the site is a fake.

Another way to verify if a website is a fake is through browsing all the menus and internal links before entering the login details. Malware creators may not go through the trouble of recreating an entire website's content.

To guard against phishing, never click on an email link to log in or change account details. Always type the known URL on the browser address bar. If clicking an email link asks the user to log in, then do not continue. Instead, type the correct URL in the browser's address bar before logging in.

The next chapter discusses other payloads that worms usually bring.

# Chapter 4 - Trojan Horse

Trojans are malware that disguise as useful programs or install together with a legitimate application. Its name comes from the Trojan War, a part of Greek mythology where a wooden gift horse had soldiers inside that attacked the enemies while they were asleep to win the war. Similarly, a Trojan pretends to be a useful application, waiting for the user to launch it to execute the malicious code. Once activated, trojans will run in the background to do their designated task.

Trojans do not replicate and spread by themselves. They often combine with worms to infect other computers. Trojans are also common on unsolicited email attachments, while some users download them along with valid applications.

There are several types of trojans according to function.

### Root kits

Root kit is not inherently bad. It is originally a tool for system administrators. It becomes bad if the creator installs it on a computer without permission from the owner, especially if the purpose is to do malicious tasks.

Some trojans will modify the computer's system for hackers to gain access. Root kits are tools for administrators that hide in the operating system while providing a back door for their creator. With privileged access, a root kit's owner can do almost anything to the infected computer remotely. Root kits are good at hiding their existence, making them difficult to detect. They can also delete any traces of malware installation. Root kits usually remain hidden until activated.

### Bots

Bots are programs that perform automated tasks. Some bots, called spambots, flood websites with spam advertisements to generate traffic for another website. This is common in online forums and is the main reason why websites validate users before accepting their registration details. Some registration forms require the user to type the characters shown on an image to validate that the applicant is human. However, some spammers go around this by hiring humans to solve the test, although it comes at a cost.

A more malicious bot is one that employs brute-force attack on target websites. Most website owners do not build websites from scratch, but simply use an open source Content Management System (CMS) as a starting point. A CMS is a fully functioning website that allows the user to update content without writing a single line of HTML code. There are many templates to choose from, and websites owners can customize further by using their own graphic images. Using CMS, owners can update website content in a few clicks.

Many CMS software have the default username "admin" and some website owners do not bother changing it. Given the default administrator name, hackers only need to guess the password to take over the website and install malicious software. If it is a popular forum, then there is a risk that hackers can steal the member database.

To attack a website, hackers write bots that log into the target website and try to log in with passwords taken from a table of common passwords as well as words from the dictionary. A website that does not limit failed logins in a given period is a good target. Using a network of zombie computers, hackers are able to brute-force attack a website using bots with minimal risk of authorities tracking the attack's mastermind.

Stolen password databases from forums are not safe, either. Using rainbow tables, hackers can use brute-force to find the matching password for a member account. Since many users employ the same username and password on all sites they register to, this allows the hackers to hack into members' accounts on other sites as well.

### Remote-controlled Bots

Malware developers can turn an infected computer into a remote-controlled bot that will perform malicious tasks, including attacking another computer. This is how they get away with Distributed Denial of Service attacks. Attackers do not use their own computers to flood a server, but instead, they use a large network of zombie computers from unsuspecting users. This also saves the attacker from bandwidth costs since the computer owner is paying for it. It also makes it difficult to track the attacker after it spreads from one computer to another.

One analysis of an affected computer shows that bots log into a chat server, waiting for commands from its master. Think of an army of sleeper bots just waiting patiently for a command to attack. Developers will typically just let an installed Trojan do nothing until they have an army of remote-controlled bots to launch a large-scale cyber-attack. The attacker then issues the command to attack from the chat server where the bots log in each time the infected computer is running.

Without good anti-malware software, the presence of a remote-controlled bot in a computer is difficult to detect since it sleeps until a command is given.

### Keylogger

Some trojans can capture keystrokes as well as mouse movements in the background without the user knowing it. Called keyloggers, these programs can serve as surveillance software for a good purpose. Some parents use it to monitor children's online activity.

Trojan keyloggers can steal passwords and other personal credentials from unsuspecting users. It can wait for specific events, like users opening a login page, before starting to record user actions and keystrokes. It then sends the log to a remote server for its master.

### Spyware

Spyware is another Trojan that collects sensitive information similar to a keylogger. However, it is not limited to monitoring key strokes to steal user credentials, but can also gather information about the user's online activity as well.

### Adware

Adware is similar to spyware, but simply records and sends users' online activity and behavior as marketing data to marketers so they can display an appropriate advertisement. Some versions will redirect browser searches to advertisements while others will replace the default search engine with an advertiser's search engine.

Adware creators write these malware for revenue generation. Adware that alters browser settings is very difficult to remove. Antivirus software can remove adware from the computer, but usually leaves the modified browser settings. Saving browser bookmarks and restoring to factory settings can sometimes fix the problem.

### Ransomware

Ransomware does what its name suggests. After installing the malicious code, it will either prevent access to the infected computer or encrypt the contents of its hard disk. Users will see a message demanding payment to disable the malware. The criminals behind typically employ money transfer services that are difficult to track. Add this to the fact that these cybercriminals usually live in other countries, making it difficult to run after them.

To spread ransomware, cybercriminals typically take over a legitimate website, usually without the owner's knowledge, to install the malware. They can also spread ransomware using drive-by downloads on the compromised website.

### Drive-by Download

A drive-by download will allow the installation of malware by simply browsing an infected website. The user does not even have to click a download link. The affected website contains codes that check for browser or operating system vulnerabilities that allow for automatic download. The malware will install a program with a task to connect to another server to download the rest of the malware. The victim may not notice the download due to the initial programs' small size.

Some anti-malware software can warn if a website has malware when a user tries to access it.

### Suspicious Packers

In order to avoid detection, suspicious packers compress and encrypt malware code. Good anti-malware utilities are aware of this and are able to detect the behavior of suspicious packers and prevent them from executing.

### Removing Trojans

Most antivirus companies have software that can automatically remove trojans. While it is possible to remove Trojans manually, this may be a challenge since many have multiple copies running that can reinstall copies if the user deletes one.

When looking for good antivirus software, try the demo versions first. If satisfied, users can pay for other features that provide complete protection to the computer. Some of these protections include email and web surfing security.

In some cases, antivirus software can remove malware from the system, but not from the browser. If removing browser add-ons and restoring to factory setting does not work, uninstall the browser and download again.

### Avoiding Installer Trojans

Among the popular sources of Trojans are free software installers. Software development costs money, and offering it free is not good for business. However, many people would prefer free over paid versions, especially when performing simple or one-time tasks. To address this, developers break down their programs by specific features, then allow third party marketers to offer them as free downloads in return for revenue to the developer. For example, one utility can convert AVI formats to MP4, while another can convert MP4 to MPG.

How can marketers earn money from offering free downloads? They get revenue by offering their services to advertisers. These marketers create installers for legitimate software, then include the option to install software from other companies. There is nothing wrong with that right, except that many users do not bother reading what they are installing. Unfortunately, many of these optional programs are adware that antivirus software tag as Potential Unwanted Programs (PUP).

An installer for free software will first confirm that users want to install the desired legitimate program. After the user clicks on the Continue or Next button, the installer will get the user's consent to install additional software along with a few descriptions of its benefits. Sometimes, the installer will display an End User License Agreement (EULA), something that no one ever reads, but simply agrees to. It is common to see more than one program added in the installation. The problem, however, is that the default buttons will install these extra programs if the user is not careful.

How can users avoid these additional installations, especially if the user is unsure if the other software is required? Most installers have a Decline button for optional installations. When an installer shows the Decline button, then that additional software is probably a PUP. Pay attention to the presence of Decline buttons.

Some installers have no separate dialog boxes for additional software installation. Instead, easy and custom install options are available, with the easy install as the default. What the user may not see is that the easy install option will sometimes install additional software. Click the custom install option when it is available and deselect unfamiliar applications.

Some antivirus may give an alert that the installer has a Trojan. Always scan the installer after downloading. Users can do this by selecting the installer, right clicking then selecting the Scan option to run the antivirus. This is also a good practice after inserting USB devices.

Users can perform additional verification after each installation. In Windows, simply select Programs and Features from the control panel, then click the Installed On tab. Sort the list in descending order. The programs with the current date are the ones included in the installation. Select suspicious programs and click uninstall. To verify applications, enter the program name in a search engine to see what it does.

# Chapter 5 – Threats on Mobile Devices

Mobile technology is now a part of people's everyday lives. Smartphones today are very powerful. They are no longer just for voice and text, but for accessing the Internet and playing games as well. Though not as efficient as personal computers, users can perform most tasks on their smartphones.

For those who require laptop capability at more portable form factor, tablets are a blessing. Those who want the small size of a phone, but with a bigger screen like a tablet, can choose a phablet. Mobile computing is now a reality.

As computers, these mobile devices can be targets of malware. To minimize these, Android and IOS, the leading mobile platforms, have screening policies in place to reduce the chances of malware getting into the official stores. Additionally, updates to the operating system often include security fixes for known vulnerabilities to strengthen the security of devices. Installing the latest updates, when available to the user's mobile device, addresses possible malware problems.

By default, users can only download apps from the official stores. This is Google Play for Android and App Store for IOS. However, a checkbox on Android's setting will allow the user to download from any external server. There lies the problem.

The price for mobile apps is quite low compared to their PC counterparts. However, many users still do not wish to pay for the apps they download, despite their low prices. Malware creators take advantage of this by making commercial apps available for free download on third party servers. By simply deselecting a default Android setting, users can now download a paid app for free.

Unfortunately, for them, these modified apps may contain malware written for mobile devices. Once installed on a mobile device and executed, these malware take over the device and do what PC malware often do. Some malware may steal user credentials while others may display unwanted advertisements. These malware can make the devices very slow, rendering them unusable. Restoring to factory settings may be the only option for some.

IOS has no checkbox to allow downloading of apps from unofficial sites, but bugs in the operating systems can allow jailbreaks. Jailbreaks are IOS hacks that allow users to customize their devices. It also allows users to install unofficial apps. Some of these apps may have malware and can compromise the device.

Malware creators are smart and can always find ways around a secure system. One company created a Windows application that allows users to download apps for free then transfer them to their IOS device. This comes with a risk, however, since some of these apps may also have malware.

Malware creators started targeting IOS developers in China. They did this by making local copies of Apple's development platform since downloading from Apple's official servers is quite slow for developers located in China. Unfortunately, the unofficial installer has malware that infects the apps they are developing. Some of these apps made their way into the App Store before they were discovered and removed.

Another malware creator took advantage of enterprise certificates. These certificates are used by companies to install their own apps on IOS devices without approval from Apple. Malware creators are tricking users to install an enterprise certificate so they can install apps with malware on victims' devices. Many users who do not understand the implications are at risk.

Apple quickly released an update to IOS that prevents this malware from installing. Those who are still using an older version of IOS can also avoid this malware by not allowing the installation of certificates unless it is from their company's IT department.

For IOS users, downloading apps only from the App Store can minimize the risk of malware. It does not mean that Android users are safer, though. Malware writers are invading Google Play by creating fake apps that mimic original apps, but with additional malware. Google has to monitor millions of apps and ensuring that apps do not have malware is not easy. There is a way to avoid potential malware, though. If an Android app asks for unnecessary permissions during installation, do not install it.

Fortunately, antivirus companies now have versions for both the IOS and Android platforms. Installing these apps will help users screen potential malware during installation, as well as remove malware that were accidentally installed.

# Conclusion

Thank you again for purchasing this book!

I hope this book was able to help you understand malware threats to prevent them from spreading.

The next step is to check your computers for signs of malware and apply the lessons in this book to avoid infections in the future.

Finally, if you enjoyed this book, please take the time to share your thoughts and post a review on Amazon. It'd be greatly appreciated!

Thank you and good luck!

# Book 2
# Quality Assurance

**By Solis Tech**

## *Software Quality Assurance Made Easy!*

.

# Table Of Contents

**Introduction....................................................................................26**

**Chapter 1 Definition Of Software Quality Assurance And Software Testing...........................................................................................27**

**Chapter 2 Introducing Software Quality Assurance Procedures To An Existing Company.....................................................................30**

**Chapter 3 Ensuring Software Quality.............................................34**

**Chapter 4 How To Develop And Run Software Testing.......................37**

**Chapter 5 Deciding When To Release The Software To Users............40**

**Chapter 6 Using Automated Testing Tools.......................................43**

**Conclusion........................................................................................46**

# Introduction

I want to thank you and congratulate you for purchasing the book, *"Quality Assurance: Software Quality Assurance Made Easy"*.

This book contains proven steps and strategies on how to implement Software Quality Assurance.

Software quality assurance evolved from the quality assurance in industrial production in the 1940s. With the introduction of computers and the development of applications, it has become an important aspect of software development. In this book, you will learn about the various concepts of software quality assurance and its application in your workplace.

Chapter 1 talks about the definitions of software quality assurance and quality control. It is necessary that you understand what it is so that you can fully grasp the other fundamental concepts. Chapter 2 discusses the ways you can implement software quality assurance in an existing environment. In Chapter 3, you will learn how you can ensure that the software produces quality outputs.

Chapter 4 teaches you how to develop and run software testing while Chapter 5 talks about the timing of the software release. In Chapter 6, you will learn about using automated testing tools.

Thanks again for purchasing this book, I hope you enjoy it!

# Chapter 1: Definition Of Software Quality Assurance And Software Testing

Software quality assurance is part of the process of software development. It includes the improvement and monitoring of the process. It also follows the processes, procedures, and standards. Furthermore, it ensures the resolution of problems discovered. In effect, it focuses on the prevention of problems.

Software testing, on the other hand, includes the operation of the application or system under controlled conditions, which must include all abnormal and normal conditions. The primary goal of software testing is to know what can go wrong when unexpected and expected scenarios occur. Its focus is on the detection of problems.

Companies differ in assigning responsibilities for quality assurance and software testing. There are organizations that combine both responsibilities to a single person or group. However, it is also common to have various teams that combine developers and testers. Project managers lead such teams. The decision to either combine or separate responsibilities depends on the company's business structure and size. Human beings or machines can perform software testing.

Some projects do not require a group of testers. The need for software testing depends on the project's context and size, the development methodology, the risks, the developers' experience and skill, and other factors. For example, a short-term, low-risk, and small project with expert developers, who know how to use test-first development or thorough unit testing, may not require software test engineers.

In addition, a small or new IT company may not have a dedicated software testing staff even its projects have a need for it. It may outsource software testing or use contractors. It may also adjust its approach on project development and management by using either agile test-first development or more experienced programmers. An inexperienced project manager may use his developers to do their own functional testing or skip thorough testing all together. This decision is highly risky and may cause the project to fail.

If the project is a huge one with non-trivial risks, software testing is important. The use of highly specialized software testers enhances the ability of the project to succeed because different people with different perspectives can offer their invaluable contribution because they have stronger and deeper skills.

In general, a software developer focuses on the technical issues to make a functionality work. On the other hand, a software test engineer focuses on what can go wrong with the functionality. It is very rare to come across a highly effective technical person, who can do both programming and testing tasks. As such, IT companies need software test engineers.

There are various reasons why software may have bugs. First, there is no communication or miscommunication as to the application's requirements. Second, the software is very complex so an inexperienced individual may have a difficult time understanding the software application. In addition, the software may be a big one and includes big databases, data communications, security complexities, different remote and local web services, and multi-tier distributed systems.

Third, there are programming errors. Fourth, the requirements of the software change because the end-user requests for them. In some cases, this end-user may not be aware of the effects of such changes, which can result in errors. The staff's enthusiasm is affected. Continuous modification requirements are a reality. Quality assurance and software test engineers must be able to plan and adapt continuous testing to prevent bugs from affecting the software.

Fifth, time pressures can be difficult to manage. Mistakes often occur during crunch times. Sixth, people involved in the project may not be able to manage their own egos. Seventh, the code has poor documentation or design. It is difficult to modify and maintain codes that are poorly written or documented. Bugs can occur if IT companies do not offer incentives for developers to write maintainable, understandable, and clear codes. Most companies offer incentives when they are able to finish the code quickly. Eighth, the use of software development tools can also result to bugs.

## *How Quality Assurance Evolved*

In 1946, the US Occupation Forces established the Quality Movement in Japan. The movement follows the research of W. Edwards Deming and the Statistical Process Control papers. The methods discussed by the research and papers pertained to industrial production. Each process of production has an output with a required specification and a verifiable main product. The Quality Control group measures the output at different production stages. It ensures that the output falls within the acceptable variances.

The Quality Assurance group does not part in the production process. It audits the process to ensure compliance with the established standards and guidelines. It gives its input for the continuous improvement of the process. In a manufacturing setup, it is easy to differentiate between quality assurance and quality control. These methods become the norm in manufacturing. Since they work in industrial production, they spawned the birth of software quality control and software quality assurance.

## *Quality Attributes Of Software*

Hewlett Packard's Robert Grady developed the common definition of the Software Quality Attributes. The FURPS model identified the following characteristics: functionality, usability, reliability, performance, and supportability (FURPS).

The functional attributes pertain to the features of the software. They answer the question about the purpose of the software instead of its use. The reason for the software's existence is different from the concerns about its reliability, look and feel, and security. The usability attributes are characteristics pertaining to user interface issues like consistency, interface aesthetics, and accessibility.

The reliability attributes include recoverability, accuracy, and availability of the system while performance attributes pertain to issues like startup time, recovery time, system response time, and information throughput. Supportability addresses issues like localizability, scalability, installation, configurability, compatibility, maintainability, adaptability, and testability. The FURPS model evolved into FURPS+ to include specification of constraints like physical, interface, implementation, and design constraints.

The Software Quality Control team tests the quality characteristics. The tests for usability and functionality occur during execution of the actual software. On the other hand, adaptability and supportability tests occur through code inspection. It is not the responsibility of the Software Quality Control or Software Quality Assurance to put the quality attributes into the software. The Software Quality Control team tests for the absence or presence of such characteristics while the Software Quality Assurance group ensures that each stakeholder follow the right standards and procedures during software execution.

In theory, the implementation of FURPS+ will overcome the problems caused by the software's intangible nature because the Software Quality Control team can measure each software attribute. For example, the amount of time it takes for programmers to fix a bug is a measure of supportability. To improve it requires the implementation of new coding standards.

The Software Quality Control group can inspect the code to ensure compliance with the coding standard while the Software Quality Assurance team can ensure that the quality control and programmer teams follow the right standards and process. It is the duty of the Software Quality Assurance group to collect and analyze the time spent on fixing the bug so that it can provide an input in terms of its usefulness to the process improvement initiative.

# Chapter 2: Introducing Software Quality Assurance Procedures To An Existing Company

The introduction of the software quality assurance procedures rely on the risks involved and the company's size. If the organization is large and the projects are high-risk, the management must consider a more formal quality assurance process. On the other hand, if the risk is lower, the implementation of quality assurance may be a step-at-a-time procedure. The processes of quality assurance maintain balance with productivity.

If the project or the company is small, an ad-hoc process may be more appropriate. The success of the software development relies on the team leaders and developers. More importantly, there must be enough communications between software testers, managers, customers, and developers. Requirement specifications must be complete, testable, and clear. There must be procedures for design and code reviews, as well as retrospectives. Common approaches used are Agile, Kaizen, and Deming-Shewhart Plan-Do-Check-Act methods.

It is important to evaluate documents, code, specifications, plans, and requirements. To do this, it is necessary to prepare issues lists, checklists, inspection meetings, and walkthroughs. This process is what IT people refer to as verification. On the other hand, validation occurs after verification and includes actual testing of the application. A walkthrough is evaluation in an informal meeting. There is no need to prepare for it.

An inspection is more formal than a walkthrough and attended by at most eight people including a reader, a recorder, and a moderator. Usually, an inspection's subject is a test plan or requirements specification so that the attendees will know the software's problems. The attendees must read the document before attending an inspection so they will find the problems prior to the meeting. It is difficult to prepare for an inspection but it is an effective and least costly way to ensure quality.

## *Testing Requirements That Must Be Considered*

The basis of black box testing is the software's functionality and requirements. A software tester need not be knowledgeable of code or internal design. White box testing, on the other hand, requires knowledge of code. It takes into consideration the code statements, paths, branches, and conditions. Unit testing requires testing of particular code modules or functions. Usually, the application developer performs it because it requires detailed knowledge of the code and program design.

API testing is testing of data exchange or messaging among systems parts. An incremental integration testing tests the application when there is a new functionality, which must be independent to work separately before it can be included in the application. The application programmer or software tester performs this type of testing. An integration testing requires the testing of the various parts of the software in order to know if they work together properly. Functional testing, on the other hand, is a kind of black box testing that focuses on the application's functional requirements. The software testers perform it.

System testing is also another type of black box testing. It includes testing of the general requirements specifications and all the various parts of the software. End-to-end testing, on the other hand, is a macro type of system testing. It includes testing the whole software in various situations that replicates real-world use. Smoke testing or sanity testing is an initial testing to know if the new version is performing well so that major testing can commence. Regression testing retests the application after some modifications or fixes.

Acceptance testing is final testing the software based on customer's specifications. Load testing is software testing under heavy loads in order to find out when the response time of the system fails or degrades. Stress testing, on the other hand, is system functional testing with unusually heavy loads, large complex queries of the database, using large numerical values, and heavy repetition of certain inputs or actions. Performance testing is testing using test or quality assurance plans.

The goal of usability testing depends on the customer or end-user. It uses techniques like surveys, user interviews, and user sessions' video recording. Software testers and developers are not the people to implement usability testing. Install/uninstall testing uses processes to test upgrade, full, or partial install/uninstall of the software. Recovery testing determines how the software can recover in catastrophic instances like hardware failures and crashes. Failover testing is another name for recovery testing.

Security testing tests how the application protects against willful damage, unauthorized access, and the likes. It uses sophisticated testing methods. Compatibility testing tests how the application performs in some environments. Exploratory testing, on the other hand, is an informal and creative testing that does not use any formal test cases or plans. Usually, software testers are new to the application. Ad-hoc testing is almost the same as exploratory testing but the software testers understand the application prior to testing.

Context-driven testing focuses on the software's intended use, culture, and environment. For example, medical equipment software has a different testing approach than a computer game. User acceptance testing determines if the application is satisfactory to the customer or end-user. Comparison testing, on the other hand, compares the software with its competitors.

Alpha testing occurs when the software is almost finished. Usually, end users perform this type of testing. Beta testing is testing when the software is finished and ready for final release. Like alpha testing, this kind of testing is for end users. Finally, mutation testing uses test cases and allows for code changes and retesting using the original test cases to discover software bugs.

## *Common Problems And Solutions In Developing Software*

Software development can encounter common problems like poor user stories or requirements, unrealistic schedule, inadequate testing, featuritis, and miscommunication. Problems can arise if there requirements are incomplete, unclear, not testable, or too general. Furthermore, if the software development has a short timetable, problems can also be evident. If the software does not pass through the testing process, the IT organization will only know of problems if the system crashes or the end users complain.

In addition, problems can arise if the users or customers request for more new functionalities even after the development goals are set. Finally, if there is miscommunication between the programmers and customers, problems are inevitable. If it is an agile project, the problems become evident when it strays away from agile principles.

If there are common problem then there are also common solutions like solid requirements, realistic schedules, adequate testing, sticking to original requirements, and communication. Software requirements must be complete, clear, cohesive, detailed, testable, and attainable. All players concerned must agree upon them. In agile environments, there must be close coordination with end users or customers so that any change in requirement is clear. There must be enough time for design, planning, bug fixing, testing, changes, retesting, and documentation. Each person must not feel burnout during the project.

For testing to be adequate, it must start early. Retesting must occur after each change or fix. There must be enough time for bug fixing and testing. If the end user or customer requests for excessive changes when development has begun, it is important that the project manager explain the consequences. If the change is important, a schedule change is inevitable to accommodate it.

The project manager must manage the expectations of the end users or customer. In an agile environment, the project manager can expect significant change in the initial requirements. There must be a schedule for inspections and walkthroughs. The use of communication tools is important to ensure cooperation and teamwork.

## *Software Quality Assurance And Software Quality Control In The Workplace*

If there is no formal implementation of Software Quality Assurance/Software Quality Control, the quality group can mirror that of an engineering services group. It performs the tasks not done by the development team. It reports to the application development manager. Under this scenario, the manager can instruct the quality assurance personnel to install a load-testing tool and declare him as a performance expert. Although the quality assurance person must perform load testing, it is the job of the software designer/programmer. As such, the software quality assurance/software quality control must be separate from the development team.

Software quality assurance requires the establishment of templates used during reviews. Such templates must have sections for both non-functional and functional requirements. For example, the requirements for performance must be in terms of transaction rates and user population. The use of Traceability Matrix can help in the requirements management. The matrix also encourages the analyst to use individual requirements for cross-referencing.

Software quality assurance verifies that the requirements comply with the templates and that they are not ambiguous. It reviews the risks of non-completion of the non-functional attributes, as well as the Traceability Matrix, to ensure usability of all requirements in other specifications. Software quality assurance can write the test cases, which refer to some of the requirements. It can cross-reference the requirements in the Traceability Matrix.

The interface specification is a requirement if the software is component-based. Software quality assurance must subject the document to verification. It must also subject other lower level specifications to quality assurance if such requirements are critical. Even if there are limited resources for software quality assurance, an IT organization can obtain a good return-on-investment if it pays attention to requirements and interfaces.

# Chapter 3: Ensuring Software Quality

Software quality is the delivery of bug-free software within budget and on time. Because quality is subjective, it depends on the customer and his overall influence in the project. A customer can be an end user, a customer contract officer, a customer acceptance tester, a customer manager, a software maintenance engineer, and others. Each customer has his own definition of quality.

A code is good if it works, is secure, bug free, maintainable, and readable. Some companies have standards, which their programmers follow. However, each developer has his own idea about what is best. Standards have different metrics and theories. If there are excessive rules and standards, they can limit creativity and productivity. A design can be functional or internal design.

An internal design is good if the overall structure of the software code is clear, easily modifiable, understandable, and maintainable. It is robust with the capability to log status and with sufficient error handling. Furthermore, the software works as expected. A functional design is good if the software functionality comes from the requirements of the end user and customer. Even an inexperienced user can use the software without reading the user manual or seeking online help.

The software life cycle starts with the conception of the application and commences when the software is no longer used. It includes factors like requirements analysis, initial concept, internal design, functional design, test planning, documentation planning, document preparation, coding, maintenance, testing, integration, retesting, updates, and phase out.

A good software test engineer must possess a test to break attitude, which means that he must be able to focus on the detail in order to ensure that the application is of good quality. He must be diplomatic and tactful so that he can maintain a good relationship with the programmers, the customers, and the managements.

It is helpful if he has previous experience on software development so that he understands the whole process deeply. A good software test engineer is able to appreciate the point of view of the programmers. He must have good judgment skills to be able to determine critical or high-risk application areas that require testing.

A good quality assurance engineer also shares the same qualities with a good software test engineer. Furthermore, he must understand the whole process of software development and the organizations' goals and business approach. He must possess understanding of all sides of issues in order to communicate effectively with everyone concerned. He must be diplomatic and patient, especially in the early stages of the quality assurance process. Lastly, he must be able to detect problems during inspections and reviews.

## *Qualities Of A Good Quality Assurance Or Test Manager*

A good manager must be familiar with the process of software development and must be enthusiastic and promote positivity in the team. He must be able to increase productivity by promoting teamwork and cooperation between quality assurance, software, and test engineers. If the processes require improvements, he must be diplomatic in ensuring smooth implementation of such changes.

He must be able to withstand pressure and offer the right feedback about quality issues to the other managers. He must be able to hire and keep the right personnel. He must possess strong communication skills to deal with everyone concerned in the process. Lastly, he must stay focused and be able to hold meetings.

## *Importance Of Documentation In Quality Assurance*

If the team is large, it is more useful to have the proper documentation for efficient communication and management of projects. Documentation of quality assurance practices is necessary for repeatability. Designs, specifications, configurations, business rules, test plans, code changes, bug reports, test cases, and user manuals must have proper documentation. A system of documentation is necessary for easy obtaining and finding of information.

Each project has its own requirements. If it is an agile project, the requirements may change and evolve. Thus, there is no need for detailed documentation. However, it is useful to document user stories. Documentation on the software requirements describes the functionality and properties of the software. It must be clear, reasonably detailed, complete, attainable, cohesive, and testable. It may be difficult to organize and determine the details but there are tools and methods that are available.

It is important to exercise care in documenting the requirements of the project's customer, who may be an outside or in-house personnel, an end user, a customer contract officer, a customer acceptance tester, a customer manager, a sales person, or a software maintenance engineer. If the project did not meet the expectations, any of these customers can slow down the project.

Each organization has its own way of handling requirements. If the project is an agile project, the requirements are in the user stories. On the other hand, for other projects, the requirements are in the document. Some organizations may use functional specification and high-level project plans. In every requirement, documentation is important to help software testers to make test plans and perform testing. Without any significant documentation, it is impossible to determine if the application meets the user expectations.

Even if the requirements are not testable, it is still important to test the software. The test results must be oriented towards providing information about the risk levels and the status of the application. It is significant to have the correct testing approach to ensure success of the project. In an agile project, various approaches can use methods that require close cooperation and interaction among stakeholders.

# Chapter 4: How To Develop And Run Software Testing

To develop the steps for software testing, it is necessary to consider the following.

First, it is important to get the requirements, user stories, internal design, functional design, and any other information that can help with the testing process.

Second, testing must have budget and schedule.

Third, it must have personnel with clear responsibilities.

Fourth, there must be project context to determine testing approaches, scope, and methods.

Fifth, identification of limitations and scope of tests is necessary in order to set priorities.

Sixth, testing must include methods and approaches applicable.

Seventh, it must have the requirements to determine the test environment.

Eighth, it must have requirements for testing tools.

Ninth, it is important to determine the data requirements for testing input.

Tenth, identification of labor requirements and tasks are important.

Eleventh, it must determine milestones, timelines, and schedule estimates.

Twelfth, testing must include error classes, boundary value analysis, and input equivalence classes, when needed.

Thirteenth, it must have a test plan and documents for approvals and reviews.

Fourteenth, testing must determine test scenarios and cases.

Fifteenth, it must include reviews, approvals of test cases, inspections, approaches, and scenarios.

Sixteenth, there must be testing tools and test environment, user manuals, configuration guides, reference documents, installation guides, test tracking processes, archiving and logging processes, and test input data.

Seventeenth, it must include software releases,

## *The Test Plan*

A test plan is a document, which includes scope, objectives, and focus of the software testing activity. To prepare it, it is important to consider the efforts needed to validate the software's acceptability. The test plan must help even those people who are not part of the test group. Testing must be thorough but not very detailed.

The test plan can include the following: the title, the software version number, the plan's revision history, table of contents, the intended audience, the goal of testing, the overview of the software, relevant documents, legal or standards requirements, identifier and naming standards, and requirements for traceability. The test plan must also include overall project organization, test organization, dependencies and assumptions, risk analysis of the project, focus and priorities of testing, limitations and scope, test outline, data input outline, test environment, analysis of test environment validity, configuration and setup of test environment, and processes for software migration among other things.

A test case includes the input, event, or action plus its expected result in order to know if software's functionality is working as planned. It contains test case identifier, objective, test case name, test setup, requirements for input data, steps, and expected results. The details may differ, depending on the project context and organization. Some organizations handle test cases differently. Most of them use less-detailed test scenarios for simplicity and adaptability of test documentation. It is important to develop test cases because it is possible to detect problems and errors in the software through them.

## *When A Bug Is Discovered*

If the software has a bug, the programmers must fix it. The software must undergo retesting after the resolution of the error. Regression testing must be able to check that the solutions performed were not able to create more problems within the application. A system for problem tracking must be set up so it becomes easier to perform the retesting. There are various software tools available to help the quality assurance team.

In tracking the problems, it is good to consider the following: complete information about the bug, bug identifier, present bug status, software version number, how the bug was discovered, specifics about environment and hardware, test case information, bug description, cause of the bug, fix description, retesting results, etc. There must be a reporting process so that the appropriate personnel will know about the errors and fixes.

A configuration management includes the various processes used to coordinate, control, and track requirements, code, problems, documentation, designs, change requests, tools, changes made, and person who made the changes. If the software has many bugs, the software tester must report them and focus on critical bugs. Because this problem can affect the schedule, the software tester must inform the managers and send documentation in order to substantiate the problem.

The decision to stop testing is difficult to do, especially for complex applications. In some cases, complete testing is not possible. Usually, the decision to stop testing considers the deadlines, the degree of test cases completion, the depletion of the test budget, the specified coverage of code, the reduction of the bug rate, and the ending of alpha or beta testing periods. If there is not enough time to perform thorough testing, it is important to focus the testing on important matters based on risk analysis. If the project is small, the testing can depend on risk analysis again.

In some cases, there are organizations that are not serious about quality assurance. For them, it is important to solve problems rather than prevent problems. Problems regarding software quality may not be evident. Furthermore, some organizations reward people who fix problems instead of incentivizing prevention of problems. Risk management includes actions that prevent things from happening. It is a shared responsibility among stakeholders. However, there must be a point person who is primarily responsible for it. In most cases, the responsibility falls on the quality assurance personnel.

# Chapter 5: Deciding When To Release The Software To Users

In most projects, the decision to release the software depends on the timing of the end testing. However, for most applications, it is difficult to specify the release criteria without using subjectivity and assumptions. If the basis of the release criteria is the result of a specific test, there is an assumption that this test has addressed all the necessary software risks.

For many projects, this is impossible to do without incurring huge expenses. Therefore, the decision is actually a leap of faith. Furthermore, most projects try to balance cost, timeliness, and quality. As such, testing cannot address the balance of such factors when there is a need to decide on the release date.

Usually, the quality assurance or test manager decides when to release the software. However, this decision involves various assumptions. First, the test manager understands the considerations, which are significant in determining the quality of the software to justify release. Second, the quality of the software may not balance with cost and timeliness. In most organization, there is not enough definition for sufficient quality. Thus, it becomes very subjective and may vary from day to day or project to project.

The release criteria must consider the sales goals, deadlines, market considerations, legal requirements, quality norms of the business segment, programming and technical considerations, expectations of end users, internal budget, impact on the other projects, and a host of other factors. Usually, the project manager must know all these factors.

Because of the various considerations, it may not be possible for the quality assurance manager or test manager to decide the release of the software. However, he may be responsible in providing inputs to the project manager, who makes the release decision. If the project or the organization is small, the decision to release the software rests on the project manager or the product manager. For larger organizations or projects, there must be a committee to decide when to release the software.

If the software requirements change continuously, it is important for all stakeholders to cooperate from the beginning so that they all understand how the change in requirements may affect the project. They may decide on alternate strategies and test plans in advance. It is also beneficial to the project if the initial design of the software can accommodate changes later on. A well-documented code makes it easier for programmers to make the necessary changes.

It is also good to use rapid prototyping if possible so that customers will not make more requests for changes because they are sure of their requirements from the very beginning. The initial schedule of the project must allow extra lead-time for these changes. If possible, all changes must be in the "Phase 2" of the software version. It is important that only easily implemented requirements must be in the project.

The difficult ones must be in the future versions. The management and the customers must know about costs, inherent risks, and scheduling impacts of big changes in the requirements. If they know about the challenges, they can decide whether to continue with the changes or not.

There must be balance between expected efforts with the effort to set up automated testing for the changes. The design of the automated test scripts must be flexible. Its focus must be on aspects of application, which will remain unchanged. The reduction of the appropriate effort for the risk analysis of the changes can be through regression testing.

The design of the test cases must be flexible. The focus must be on ad-hoc testing and not on detailed test cases and test plans. If there is a continuous request for changes in the requirements, it is unreasonable to expect that requirements will remain stable and pre-determined. Thus, it may be appropriate to use approaches for agile development.

It is difficult to determine if software has significant hidden or unexpected functionality. It also indicates that the software development process has deeper problems. The functionality must be removed if does not serve any purpose to the software because it may have unknown dependencies or impacts. If not removed, there must be a consideration for the determination of regression testing needs and risks. The management must know if there are significant risks caused by the unexpected functionality.

The implementation of quality assurance processes is slow over time because the stakeholders must have a consensus. There must be an alignment of processes and organizational goals. As the organization matures, there will be an improvement on productivity. Problem prevention will be the focus. There will be a reduction of burnout and panics. There will be less wasted effort and more improved focus.

The processes must be efficient and simple to prevent any "Process Police" mentality. Furthermore, quality assurance processes promote automated reporting and tracking thereby minimizing paperwork. However, in the short run, implementation may be slow. There will be more days for inspections, reviews, and planning but less time for handling angry end users and late night fixing of errors.

If the growth of the IT organization is very rapid, fixed quality assurance processes may be impossible. Thus, it is important to hire experienced people. The management must prioritize issues about quality and maintain a good relationship with the customers. Every employee must know what quality means to the end user.

# Chapter 6: Using Automated Testing Tools

If the project is small, learning and implementing the automated testing tools may not be worth it. However, these automated testing tools are important for large projects. These tools use a standard coding language like Java, ruby, python, or other proprietary scripting language. In some cases, it is necessary to record the first tests for the generation of the test scripts. Automated testing is challenging if there are continuous changes to the software because a change in test code is necessary every time there is a new requirement. In addition, the analysis and interpretation of results can be difficult.

Data driven or keyword driven testing is common in functional testing. The maintenance of actions and data is easy through a spreadsheet. The test drivers read the information for them to perform the required tests. This strategy provides more control, documentation, development, and maintenance of test cases. Automated tools can include code analyzers, coverage analyzers, memory analyzers, load/performance test tools, web test tools, and other tools.

A test engineer, who does manual testing, determines if the application performs as expected. He must be able to judge the expected outcome. However, in an automated test, the computer judges the test outcome. A mechanism must be present for the computer to compare automatically between the actual and expected outcomes for every test scenario. If the test engineer is new to automated testing, it is important that he undergo training first.

Proper planning and analysis are important in selecting and using an automated tool for testing. The right tool must be able to test more thoroughly than manual methods. It must test faster and allow continuous integration. It must also reduce the tedious manual testing. The automation of testing is costly. However, it may be able to provide savings in the long term.

## *Choosing The Appropriate Test Environment*

There is always a tradeoff between cost and test environment. The ultimate scenario is to have a collection of test environments, which mirror exactly all possible usage, data, network, software, and hardware characteristics that the software can use. For most software, it is impossible to predict all environment variations. Furthermore, for complex and large systems, it is extremely expensive to duplicate a live environment.

The reality is that decisions on the software environment characteristics are important. Furthermore, the choice of test environments takes into consideration logistical, budget, and time constraints. People with the most technical experience and knowledge, as well as with the deep understanding of constraints and risks, make these decisions. If the project is low risk or small, it is common to take the informal approach. However, for high risk or large projects, it is important to take a more formalize procedure with many personnel.

It is also possible to coordinate internal testing with efforts for beta testing. In addition, it is possible to create built-in automated tests upon software installation by users. The tests are able to report information through the internet about problems and application environment encountered. Lastly, it is possible to use virtual environments.

## *The Best Approach To Test Estimation*

It is not easy to find the best approach because it depends on the IT organization, the project, as well as the experience of the people involved. If there are two projects with the same size and complexity, the right test effort for life-critical medical software may be very large compared to a project involving an inexpensive computer game. The choice of a test estimation approach based on complexity and size may be applicable to a project but not to the other one.

The implicit risk context approach caters to a quality assurance manager or project manager, who uses risk context with past personal experiences to allocate resources for testing. The risk context assumes that each project is similar to the others. It is an experience-based intuitive guess.

The metrics-based approach, on the other hand, uses past experiences on different projects. If there is already data from a number of projects, the information is beneficial in future test planning. For each new project, the basis of adjustment of required test time is the available metrics. In essence, this is not easy to do because it is judgment based on historical experience.

The test-work breakdown approach decomposes the testing tasks into smaller tasks to estimate testing with a reasonable accuracy. It assumes that the breakdown of testing tasks is predictable and accurate and that it is feasible to estimate the testing effort. If the project is large, this is not feasible because there is a need to extend testing time if there are many bugs. In addition to, there is a need to extend development time.

The iterative approach is for large test projects. An initial rough estimate is necessary prior to testing. Once testing begins and after finishing a small percentage of testing work, there is a need to update the testing estimate because testers have already obtained additional knowledge of the issues, risks, and software quality. There is also a need to update test schedules and plans. After finishing a larger percentage of testing work, the testing estimate requires another update. The cycle continues until testing ends.

The percentage-of-development approach requires a quick way of testing estimation. If the project has 1,000 hours of estimated programming effort, the

IT firm usually assigns a 40% ratio for testing. Therefore, it will allot 400 hours for testing. The usefulness of this approach depends on risk, software type, personnel, and complexity level.

In an agile software development approach, the test estimate is unnecessary if the project uses pure test-driven development although it is common to mix some automated unit tests with either automated or manual functional testing. By the nature of agile-based projects, they are not dependent on testing efforts but on the construction of the software.

# Conclusion

Thank you again for purchasing this book!

I hope this book was able to help you to understand the concepts of Software Quality Assurance.

The next step is to apply what you learned from this book to your work.

Finally, if you enjoyed this book, please take the time to share your thoughts and post a review on Amazon. It'd be greatly appreciated!

Thank you and good luck!

www.ingramcontent.com/pod-product-compliance
Lightning Source LLC
Chambersburg PA
CBHW060929050326
40689CB00013B/3019

* 9 7 8 1 5 2 3 8 6 6 9 4 6 *